HW

AT HOME IN WORLD WAR TWO

PROPAGANDA

Stewart Ross

941.084

IMPERIAL WAR MUSEUM

Evans

Evans Brothers Limited

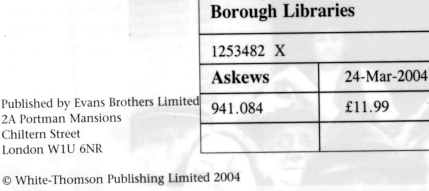

"... strictly between these four walls!"

CARELESS TALK COSTS LIVES

Published by Evans Brothers Limited
2A Portman Mansions
Chiltern Street
London W1U 6NR

© White-Thomson Publishing Limited 2004

Produced for Evans Brothers Limited by White-Thomson Publishing Ltd
2/3 St Andrew's Place, Lewes, East Sussex BN7 1UP

Printed in Dubai

Editor: Philippa Smith
Consultant and Picture Researcher: Terry Charman, Historian,
Research and Information Department, Imperial War Museum
Designer: Christopher Halls, Mind's Eye Design Ltd, Lewes
Proofreader: Rosemary Ashley

British Library Cataloguing in Publication Data
  Ross, Stewart
  Propaganda. – (At Home in World War Two)
  1. World War, 1939–45 – Propaganda – Juvenile literature
  2. World War, 1939–45 – Social aspects – Great Britain – Juvenile literature
  I. Title
  941'.084
  ISBN 0 237 52584 4

Captions:
Cover and this page: A cartoon by the artist Fougasse, warning people to take care
what they say in case enemy spies are listening – the face in the painting is Hitler's!
Cover (centre): People kept up with the war's progress by reading newspaper reports
although they knew that, because of government censorship, the information they
were being given was not always accurate.
Cover (background): A mountain of aluminium pots and pans donated by the public in
the summer of 1940 in response to a BBC radio appeal by Lord Beaverbrook, Minister
of Aircraft Production, for 'Saucepans for Spitfires'. They were to be melted down and
used in aircraft production.
Title page: People of Lambeth Walk, giving their 'Oi' sign after a German night air
raid in September 1940. The Government approved of photographs like this, which
showed people's ability to remain positive in spite of danger and hardship.
Contents page: The clever wartime hoarding on Nelson's Column, Trafalgar Square,
London, links Britain's allies – the USSR (Russia) and the USA – to the British
people (US) and each individual (U), urging everyone to save money.

For sources of quoted material see page 31.

CONTENTS

HEARTS AND MINDS

All Britons were involved in World War Two (1939–45), whether they wanted to be or not. Those in the Army, Royal Navy or Royal Air Force were in the front line, but the part played by others was just as important. They had to protect the country against air raids and be prepared to defend it against invasion; their work and co-operation produced the nation's food, weapons, ships and aircraft; and all this hardship and suffering lasted six long years.

Britain fought on the side of France, Belgium, the Netherlands, Poland and other countries. They fought against Germany and, later, Italy. In 1941, Russia and the USA joined the war on Britain's side, forming the Allies, and Japan sided with Germany and Italy. This spread the fighting right around the world. The war finally ended with an allied victory in 1945.

▼ *Just the sort of cheery photograph the Government liked: householders in north-west England gather in their street for a sing-song around a piano saved from a bomb-damaged house.*

THE PATH TO WAR

Adolf Hitler became leader of Germany in 1933. Backed by his Nazi Party, he removed those who opposed him and began to take over neighbouring countries. After Germany took over Czechoslovakia, Britain and France promised to support anyone else threatened by Nazi aggression. On 1 September 1939, Hitler invaded Poland. Two days later, Britain and France declared war on Germany.

◀ *Responding to the 'Dig for Victory' campaign, a work party arrives on Hampstead Heath, London, ready for a day's work on the allotments.*

Britain's war effort was successful partly because people's morale – their mood or spirit – remained quite high. Like members of a good football team, people were focused on victory. Keeping up morale was a vital government task. If most British people had not believed they could win, especially in 1940, defeat would have followed.

To maintain morale and get people to behave the way it wanted, the Government and other agencies, such as newspapers, used propaganda. Propaganda, like advertising, is information and opinion that supports a particular point of view. Wartime propaganda took many forms: radio broadcasts, posters, booklets, films, newspaper reports and articles, and advertisements – anything, in fact, to influence the hearts and minds of the people.

USE SPADES NOT SHIPS

GROW YOUR OWN FOOD
AND SUPPLY YOUR OWN COOKHOUSE

▶ *A poster encouraging people to grow their own food and so reduce the need to import it by ship. Shipping was in constant danger of attack by enemy aircraft and submarines.*

THE SECRET WEAPON

BETTER POT-LUCK

with Churchill today

THAN HUMBLE PIE

under Hitler tomorrow

DON'T WASTE FOOD!

▲ *This poster shows the way the Government used humour and the familiar image of Winston Churchill to get its message across. At the same time it poked fun at Hitler.*

▶ *By the end of the war there was hardly a street in the country that did not have a government poster somewhere in it. These posters, urging people to save money and fuel, and volunteer for war work, appeared late in the war when the country faced severe shortages.*

Propaganda, like advertising, is most powerful when people do not realise they are being influenced. For this reason it is rarely straightforward. During the war it involved filtering or altering news and opinions so people learned only what the Government wanted them to learn.

The British Government could, if it wished, censor all newspapers and other publications (see pages 14–15). It could also control the BBC, Britain's only wartime radio service (see page 20). In this way, although it was not obvious, the Government supervised the news.

Encouraged by the Ministry of Information, on 31 May 1940 the *Daily Express* tried to put a brave face on Britain's defeat in France:

'Men Fight Metal
No country has a right to ask for such heroism as our fighting men have freely given ...The B.E.F. [British Expeditionary Force in France] carry out the greatest rearguard action ever fought in history ... Brave men face an overwhelming mass of metal and machinery. Yet such is their valour that Hitler has to throw a million troops against them.'

Humour was another important part of wartime propaganda, especially in Britain. It was used to mock or make light of a serious situation. Prime Minister Churchill, for instance, always mispronounced the name 'Nazi' ('Nar-tzi') as 'Narhzee'. This insult gave the impression that he did not take the enemy seriously.

The German leader Adolf Hitler (inset) was brilliant at giving highly emotional speeches to large rallies of his supporters (main picture).

Another feature of wartime propaganda was repetition. This involved saying something time and time again until people believed it. Hitler told the German people they were a master race so often that many thought it must be true.

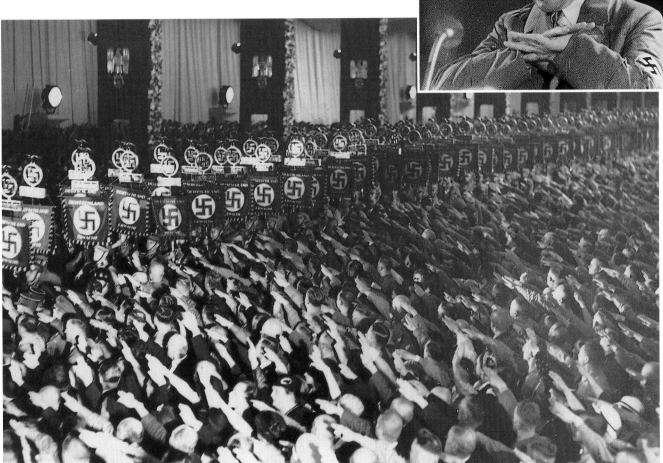

At first, German propaganda, organised by Joseph Goebbels, was more effective than British. Goebbels was particularly good at using mass rallies and films to make the Germans feel proud of themselves. In contrast, early material from Britain's Ministry of Information was often seen as bossy (see page 9) and boring (see page 27).

NAZI IMAGE-MAKER

Highly educated and ruthlessly ambitious, Joseph Goebbels (1897–1945) was Minister of Propaganda in Nazi Germany. Like his master, Adolf Hitler, he was a powerful speaker, and he ran his ministry with terrifying skill. His clever use of repeated images and phrases in rallies and the media helped persuade the German people to support Hitler's policies.

'WE SHALL NEVER SURRENDER'

Despite the defeat of British forces in France in May 1940, and their withdrawal from Dunkirk, the mood in Britain was surprisingly upbeat in view of what would seem to have been a desperate situation.

▶ *This photograph of defeated British soldiers returning from France in 1940 suggests they remained cheerful. In fact, as most of them were depressed and exhausted, this picture probably shows their relief at arriving home safely.*

▼ *A poster that deliberately suggests civilians (Churchill) and servicemen and women (as in the aircraft) can work together for victory.*

Nothing, it seemed, could stand in the way of the Nazi advance, but Prime Minister Winston Churchill, in a speech to Parliament on 4 June 1940, almost single-handedly convinced the nation that this was not so:

> 'Even though large tracts of Europe and many old and famous states have fallen or may fall into the grip of the Gestapo and all the odious apparatus of Nazi rule, we shall not flag or fail. We shall go on to the end. We shall fight in France, we shall fight in the seas and oceans, we shall fight with growing confidence and growing strength in the air; we shall defend our island, whatever the cost may be. We shall fight on the beaches, we shall fight on the landing-grounds, we shall fight in the fields and in the streets, we shall fight in the hills; we shall never surrender.'

◀ Children as well as adults answered the call for volunteers to aid the war effort. These schoolgirls gave up two weeks' holiday to work in an army supply depot.

In a few lines Churchill derides the enemy ('grip of the Gestapo', 'odious apparatus of Nazi rule') and outlines the future conflict. His use of 'island' suggests a fortress. By saying 'we' many times, he is creating a sense of unity, implying (with doubtful accuracy) that the whole nation is determined to resist. Similarly, 'shall' leaves no room for doubt, although there were many doubters at the time. Finally, two phrases – 'we shall not … fail' and 'fight with growing confidence and growing strength in the air' – offer hope of eventual victory.

Surprisingly, Churchill was not very interested in the official propaganda produced by his Ministry of Information. Speeches like that opposite, however, and the one he made before the Battle of Britain, which he said would be the country's 'finest hour', were brilliant propaganda.

▶ No humour here, but a stark and serious message from the Prime Minister to the British public.

DESERVE VICTORY!

Some newspapers were urging last-ditch resistance even before Churchill did so:

'The British people know now that they are fighting for their existence. Either we awaken every energy in our being or this soil of England will be drenched by blood and unending tears.'

Evening Standard, 10 May 1940

Propaganda to get women to work: *'If you are working for export, you are working for victory!'*

'Nearly half of our food comes across the sea … Now, here is your part in the fight for victory. When a particular food is not available, cheerfully accept something else.'

Ministry of Food, 1941

SWEETENING THE PILL

There were two reasons for withholding news of the war: either it might contain information that would help the enemy, or it was so bad that it would damage morale.

During the Battle of Britain, and the Blitz, when British cities were being bombed night after night, the new device known as radar enabled Britain's air defences to track incoming enemy aircraft with great accuracy. Although a triumph for British science and engineering, radar was not mentioned in the news. This was to stop the enemy learning of its usefulness, and to prevent their bombers targeting radar stations.

Britain generally reported bad news, but very carefully. When most of the news was bad (1940–41), the Ministry of Information found this especially difficult.

Prime Minister to Minister of Information, 26 July 1940: *'The Press and broadcast should be asked to handle air raids in a cool way and on a diminishing tone of public interest. The facts should be chronicled without undue prominence to headlines. The people should be accustomed to treat air raids as a matter of ordinary routine. Localities affected should not be mentioned with any precision. Photographs showing shattered houses should not be published unless there is something very peculiar about them, or to illustrate how well the shelters work. It must be clear that the vast majority of people are not at all affected by any single air raid ... Everyone should learn to take air raids and air-raid alarms as if they were no more than thunderstorms. Pray try to impress this upon the newspaper authorities, and persuade them to help.'*

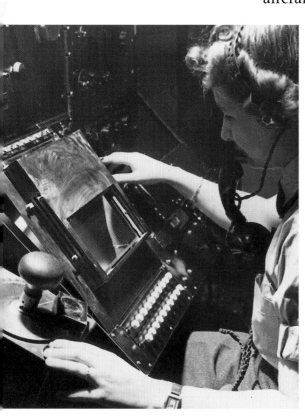

▲ A WAAF (Women's Auxiliary Air Force) radar operator at work.

By the end of the war, the Ministry had sent some 5,000 detailed notices to newspapers and the BBC, explaining what they might and might not say. Not surprisingly, different newspapers often carried very similar articles.

Bad news could be hidden by giving it little attention. A defeat could be presented as something that was bound to happen but which was much less awful than expected because of the bravery of the troops. This was how Dunkirk was explained.

Another way to make the bad news of defeat sound better was to exaggerate the enemy's cruel actions. This tactic, turning the war into a struggle of good versus evil, was often used when covering defeats in the Far East at the hands of the Japanese.

The front page of the *Daily Express*, in December 1941, shows how the disaster of the surrender of Hong Kong (a British colony in the Far East) on Christmas Day 1941 was presented as heroic, and how it was balanced by other stories:

'Hong Kong, fighting to the death with swarms of Japanese who landed yesterday at many points on the island, rejected with scorn a third offer of surrender terms ...'

'Jap Bombers Kill Children'

'Germans lose 22,000 men in six days'

'5,000 Italians drowned'

▲ 'There's not much left of Leslie's home, but he makes sure that what is left will be British.' The Government allowed pictures like this to be published because they underlined the idea that people's spirit could not be broken.

U-Boat Leaves 83 British Evacuees to Drown in Storm

NAZIS TORPEDO MERCY SHIP, KILL CHILDREN

◄ Here, the Daily Sketch uses a report of the sinking of a ship to reinforce the image of the enemy as heartless barbarians.

STRENGTH IN ADVERSITY

▲ King George VI (in army uniform) and Queen Elizabeth visit people whose homes have been bombed. The royal family and the Government were eager to show that the royals were helping in the war effort as much as anyone else.

Propaganda often tried to turn a difficult situation to advantage. The British Government and media managed this most effectively during the Blitz. When London was bombed, the Ministry of Information did not attempt to hide the extent of the raids or the damage. The *Daily Express* on 12 September 1940 reported:

> 'Total casualties on Monday night are now reported to be in the neighbourhood of 400 killed and 1,400 injured.'

Nevertheless, the Ministry made sure that good news and stories of bravery and humour received better coverage on the radio and in the newspapers. The number of enemy planes shot down, for example, was always given priority over the casualty figures. There was no mention of the fact that the King and Queen, visiting the badly damaged East End of London the morning after a raid, were supposed to have been booed by Cockneys who had not been given adequate air-raid shelters.

▶ Any photograph with a Union Jack in it – here hung from a lamppost by exhausted firefighters in Plymouth – was eagerly used by the press because it suggested patriotism.

◄ Reporting of the massive bombing raid on Coventry, which destroyed the city centre, emphasised how inhuman the enemy were to cause so much damage to a non-military target.

Government propaganda even tried to make the most of the devastating attack on Coventry on 15 November 1940. Reports made out that the air raid was somehow inhuman (although allied raids on Germany later in the war were far more horrific). They focused on injury to children, the bravery of the firefighters and people's determination not to be down-hearted.

▼ This poster aimed to maintain public confidence in the railways. It was issued in the winter of 1939–40, when the black-out began to make an impact on people's lives.

'In every heart there is no fear, only a most passionate hatred of the enemy, and a determination to carry on at all costs.'

Daily Herald report from Coventry, 16 November 1940

'The firemen were at the forefront of danger. Where the flames were, where the bombs fell. They fought the greatest fire attack ever launched: they fought it on land and water, by night and day.'

Front Line 1940–41, a Ministry of Information book about the Blitz

Despite all the brave words, there were plenty of Britons who would willingly have made peace. Molly Stevenson, a young Londoner with two small children, whose husband was in the Navy, remembers:

'I don't think we were quite so brave as everyone makes out now. Lots of people wanted it to stop and they didn't mind how – my neighbour, for a start.'

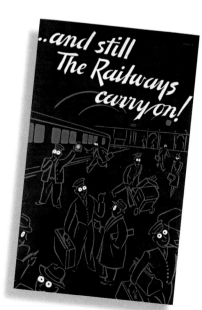

..and still The Railways carry on!

CENSORSHIP

▼ This Fougasse poster warns that enemy spies (indicated by the faces of Hitler) may be listening in to phone calls. Government censors sometimes tapped telephones, too.

"........ but for Heaven's sake don't say I told you!"

CARELESS TALK COSTS LIVES

Phyllis Pearsall, a skilled map maker, was sent to work as a censor because she spoke several foreign languages:

'Censorship was in the Prudential buildings off Holborn [London], which was quite nice for me because my own office was there, too. We were supposed to be censoring all letters that came through, but the person in charge of our table thought some of them sent to or from neutral countries needn't be. I disagreed after I had read one or two. Information was getting through to Germany about the resistance movement and people's lives were being lost.

'I reported it to the head of my department but he didn't think there was anything wrong.'

Phyllis was using the emergency powers that Parliament gave the Government in 1939. As well as controlling the content of the BBC, newspapers, periodicals, films and plays, censors were allowed to read overseas mail and tap telephones, although people didn't know their calls were being listened to.

▶ The Government strongly disapproved of the Daily Mirror cartoon by Zec, printed on 6 March 1942. The paper claimed the cartoon urged careful use of petrol that had to be brought to Britain at great risk to sailors; the Government said the cartoon was an attack on oil companies' profits implying that sailors were losing their lives so that petrol companies could increase their profits.

"The price of petrol has been increased by one penny."—Official.

Certain pieces of information, such as Churchill's movements and the names of damaged (or undamaged) factories, could not be mentioned. The names of casualties and missing persons could not be published either, nor could weather forecasts, as they might alert the enemy of a clear, moonlit night just right for an air raid. There was even an order from the Ministry of Information regarding 'Your Stars' columns in the newspapers: predictions could speak of present difficulties in Britain but they had to prophesy that all would be well in the end!

In January 1941 the Government closed the *Daily Worker*, a communist newspaper that said business people were using the war to make money, while the working classes suffered. Many people felt uneasy about the Government's decision, because Britain claimed to be fighting to preserve free speech.

▲ The results of a raid on Camden Town, London. Censors rarely allowed photographs of serious bomb damage like this to be published.

Censorship in action: the names of individuals were replaced with thick black lines:

Washington, Thursday
'New U.S. Envoy Accused: "Associated with enemy agents"
Senator ———— a Republican, in the Senate today described the appointment of ———— as United States Minister to ———— as "despicable ...
He charged ———— with having a close association with Japanese agents ... Senator ———— had previously described ———— as "wholly unfit for any high position.'"

Daily Telegraph, 15 January 1943

▶ The British were hungry for news during the war, although newspapers were censored by the Government, and did not always tell the whole story.

POSTERS AND NOTICES

Ministry of Information propaganda was direct and indirect. Newspaper reports, censored by the Ministry of Information to say what the ministry wanted, were an example of indirect propaganda. Direct propaganda included government announcements on the BBC (in those days there was no TV or commercial radio) and, most common of all, posters, leaflets and newspaper notices.

▲ The Government as nanny: posters like this were issued not because the Government wanted people to be fit for their own sakes, but because it needed their labour.

Government notice in the *Daily Express* of 1 June 1942:

'People of Britain must learn this
IF YOU KNOW...
... exactly where a bomb fell
... what time it fell
... what the bomb just missed
... how many aeroplanes there were
... what they were trying to hit
... which direction they came from
... which district they were over
... KEEP IT TO YOURSELF
and make others do the same.'

▶ (Far right) A government poster asking people to limit their travel, so as to leave the trains free for troop movements.

▶ The 'squander [waste] bug' was shown as a large beetle (with Hitler's haircut) covered in swastikas, encouraging people to waste money on things they didn't really need.

Leaflets were used mostly to pass on information. In 1939, for example, each household was sent five ARP (Air-Raid Precautions) leaflets. Some leaflets were so long and full of detailed orders, hints and tips, they were left unread.

Posters were a more effective way of getting messages across. There were three broad categories of poster: (1) giving information ('Women Required for Motor Driving'); (2) urging people to do something ('Don't Take More Than You Can Eat'); (3) warning ('Always Carry Your Gas Mask').

The most effective poster propaganda used catchy slogans ('Careless Talk Costs Lives'), striking pictures ('Keep Mum She's Not So Dumb'), humour ('Coughs and Sneezes Spread Diseases'), and endless repetition to 'wage war on waste'. Waste of all kinds was strongly discouraged.

'Food is a munition of war, don't waste it.'

Ministry of Food, 1941

'How to make rations for one go f-u-r-t-h-e-r.'

Government notice in *The People*, 29 April 1945

'ENEMY SHIPS TORPEDOED with the help of old rags. It sounds impossible doesn't it? But the charts that guide our submarine commanders are made from old rags.'

Government notice in the *Daily Mail*, 17 June 1944

'The "Squander Bug" works for Hitler!'

Government notice in the *Daily Telegraph*, 18 May 1943

By 1943 the nation's newspapers were running out of money. Fewer firms were advertising and production costs were rising. The Government came to the rescue, buying 30 per cent of their advertising space. At a cost of about £200,000 a month, people were bombarded with countless government notices on such varied subjects as 'Potato Pete's' recipes, saving money, and not wasting supplies of coal, gas and electricity.

▲ *A great deal of time, money and effort was spent persuading people to conserve resources and recycle every available scrap of food and other material. Interestingly, we are beginning to experience similar campaigns nowadays, but for very different reasons.*

WHITE AND BLACK

Most propaganda was quite straightforward and obvious: cut waste, observe the black-out, Hitler is crazy, and so on. People knew where it had come from and what its message was. Propaganda like this is known as 'white' propaganda.

There is a different, more subtle type of propaganda. This 'black' propaganda pretends to be what it is not. A good example was the printing of leaflets in Britain but in the German language and on German paper that said 'Down with Hitler!' British and American aircraft dropped these over Germany to confuse the German people – to make them wonder if the leaflets were evidence of a genuine anti-Nazi movement in Germany.

▼ *Propaganda from the air: a selection of leaflets that the RAF dropped over enemy-held territory during the war. They are in many languages, including German, French, Danish, Dutch, Belgian, Polish and Czech.*

Britain's black propaganda was organised by a special government department, the Political Warfare Executive (PWE). This was set up in August 1941 to direct propaganda operations against Germany and the enemy-occupied lands. It used many tactics to disrupt life in Germany, including printing forged stamps, banknotes, ration books, and leave [holiday] passes for German troops. A particularly subtle idea was printing editions of the German army newspaper that contained grossly exaggerated reports of the weakness of the Allies. This led German soldiers, who knew the reports could not be true, to mistrust their own newspaper.

'*This is war with the gloves off.*'

Rex Leeper of the Political War Executive

PWE's own radio station, GS1, beamed propaganda across Europe, particularly into Germany. Its black propaganda, pretending to come from within Germany, was so laced with lies that it shocked even the British Government. Goebbels, and other Nazi officials, did know it was British, but did not allow it to be mentioned in the German media for fear of attracting listeners.

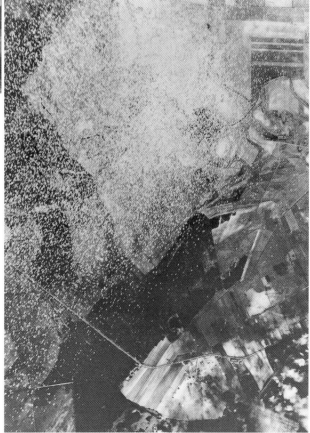

◀ *Each of these huge canisters contained thousands of leaflets that the US Army Air Force dropped over enemy-occupied territory. They were designed to confuse the Germans, encourage resistance and warn of future air raids.*

Freedom to listen!
'One of the chief blessings of democracy is that it gives us liberty. Liberty to speak – to criticise if we think fit. Liberty to listen – to both sides of an argument. We shouldn't neglect this great advantage.'

Advertisement for Murphy radios, 1944

▶ *Down they go! Clouds of British propaganda leaflets flutter down over a German manufacturing town.*

THE BBC

The British Broadcasting Company was set up in 1922. In 1927 it received a charter from the Government and became the British Broadcasting Corporation (BBC), and operated independently. When war broke out the Government gave itself the power to take over the BBC. However, it chose not to do so because the BBC was careful to follow the Government's wishes.

Working in the BBC newsroom was a highly skilled job that involved more than just writing clearly:

> 'The marshalling [collecting] of facts into concise, intelligible form, which gave the literal, accurate truth without letting slip any word which would give the listening enemy the slightest satisfaction, was not easy.'

A book published immediately after the war still insisted that the BBC told only the truth, the Nazis mostly lies.

> 'Nazi propaganda lies heard over the air could ... be immediately refuted [denied], and by a constant watch on what other people were saying, the BBC would counteract by giving us the truth.'

▲ *Prime Minister Winston Churchill spent hours carefully writing and preparing the delivery of his wartime speeches.*

▶ *Every evening the Metcalfe family, like millions of others across Britain, gathered together and tuned in to the BBC's radio news broadcast.*

'Listening to the BBC news was like a sort of ritual – everyone did it.'

May Blessed of Bedfordshire, who was a schoolgirl during the war.

Time was always available for ministers to broadcast. At 8.15 each morning there was a programme telling people how to make the most of their food rations. News was accurately reported, although in such a way as not to damage morale (see page 10), and there were always plenty of cheery programmes to keep up people's spirits.

◀ An episode of ITMA being broadcast. ITMA stood for 'It's That Man Again', the radio comedy hit show that did so much to keep people laughing during the long, grim years of war.

The BBC paid the entertainer Wilfred Pickles to change his travelling chat show into a propaganda exercise:

'It disturbed me to have to go into canteens of great industrial firms and ordnance [weapons] works and work up a frenzy of patriotism, national fervour and "go-to-it" spirit among the overalled, grease-stained men and women. I hated the job. There were marching songs and sentimental melodies and I would interview these folks about their war jobs. I had to ask such questions as: "Are we afraid of Hitler?" and "Can we lick him?", which would be followed by a united decisive roar. And there were the personal endeavour stories in which a young mother told us about her own effort. "Looking after three children and still doing a grand job in the factory. Good lass," I would say, giving her a pat on the back. How I loathed it, and how embarrassed I felt.'

◀ Vera Lynn, known as 'the Forces' Sweetheart', sings to factory workers during their lunch break. A visit from a star singer was an important way of keeping up workers' morale.

'A good laugh kept you going better than anything else.'

Lil Lawrence from Kent

CINEMA

Cinemas, selling 30 million tickets each week, were the most popular wartime recreation. Each show included a main film, a second film (known as the 'B movie'), a news film, and other short reels of information and advertising. It was, therefore, an ideal place for propaganda.

The Ministry of Information censored all films. It also set up its own film-making organisation, the Crown Film Unit. This made earnest documentaries or semi-fictional documentaries that emphasised British bravery, humour and ingenuity.

▲ *Queues outside a cinema and News Theatre, a key source of information before the days of television.*

▼ *A presentation copy from Churchill of the film* Desert Victory, *about the Battle of El Alamein (one of the first British victories of the war), ready for despatch to General Montgomery.*

'We had, I believe, seventeen tanks and I was able to borrow three of them to show our great tank force grinding round Parliament Square, the number plates and the drivers being changed for each circuit.'

Kenneth Clark, Head of the Films Division of the Ministry of Information.

Some of the Crown Unit's many high-quality films included *Target for Tonight, Coastal Command, Close Quarters* and *Fires Were Started*. Other companies made wartime films too – *The Way Ahead* (see page 23) praised the common soldier, and *Millions Like Us* was about women working in factories.

Perhaps the most famous British wartime film, about the Royal Navy and again with a strong propaganda element, was *In Which We Serve*. Using the technique of flashbacks, the film tells the grim wartime story of the British warship HMS *Torrin*.

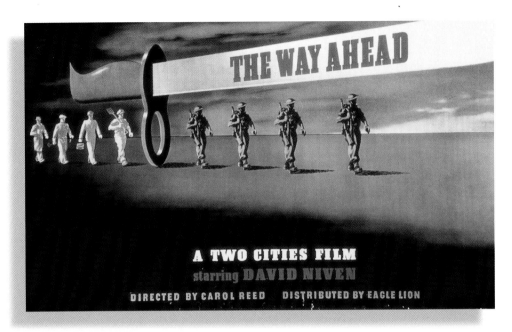

A poster advertising the wartime film The Way Ahead, *starring David Niven.*

Too much propaganda ... *'I've just seen Bette Davis's film, Now, Voyager, and what enjoyment and what relief – no war.'*

Letter to a local paper, 1944

Hollywood was making anti-Nazi films, like Charlie Chaplin's *The Great Dictator*, even before the US joined the war (December 1941). From then on it turned out hundreds of propaganda movies with titles like *Days of Glory*, *Hitler's Children*, John Ford's *They Were Expendable*, and *None Shall Escape* (about Nazi officers).

Such films played to packed cinemas all over Britain. Each, directly or indirectly, relayed the same message. By praising the Allies and scorning the enemy, they were probably as effective propaganda as anything put out by the Government.

The pictures [cinema] is the one event in the week which the factory girls really do look forward to and enjoy.'

A munitions worker, 1943

'Ark Royal [an aircraft carrier] Is Star of New Film "SHIPS WITH WINGS", the picture which opens at the Gaumont Theatre, Haymarket, on Sunday, is a thrilling exposition of the part played in this war by the Ark Royal, sunk again and again by German propaganda, but still fighting gloriously.'

Daily Express, 7 November 1941

▶ *Shooting a scene on submarine HMS* Tyrant, *for the film* Close Quarters.

GERMANY CALLING!

German propaganda directed against Britain mostly took the form of printed material dropped from aircraft, and radio broadcasts. From mid-1940 onwards, printed German propaganda had little effect.

'German-controlled Calais radio at 4.30 pm:
If what the RAF showed us is its best we cannot help laughing, and Berlin has certainly nothing to worry about. A little isolated damage can be seen in the capital.
'FACT: The RAF raid was heavier than the Luftwaffe's [the German air force] greatest attack on Britain…

Daily Express, 19 January 1943

Some Britons found the German radio broadcasts contained more news coverage and were more interesting than the restricted information released by the BBC. As Britain claimed to be fighting for freedom, the Government never made it illegal to listen to German radio. However, this was not the case in Germany, where listening to enemy broadcasts was banned.

Propaganda and reality:
'They said we [the Germans] were winning. I saw Hamburg flattened.'

Jan Hunter, who lived in the German city of Hamburg during the war

'Lord Haw-Haw?
I think I listened only once. It was ridiculous nonsense and everyone knew it.'

Marjorie Bliss, who worked at Stoke Mandeville Hospital

Haw-Haw Talk
"'This is Jarmany calling. This is Jarmany calling." That was the la-di-dah way he spoke.'

Janet Baird from Essex

▼ Another ship 'sunk by Goebbels'! The armed merchant ship Aurania lying safely in a Scottish port, after having been sunk according to a German radio broadcast.

Germany warning

'The official German wireless … announcer then said that Britain, by the erection of barricades and the fortification of towns, and by trying to turn her citizens into riflemen, "seems to have forgotten that only non-military objectives and open towns are being spared. She will, therefore, have to bear the full consequences of aerial warfare."'

Daily Telegraph, 19 June 1940

British Soldiers!
You are fighting and dying far away from your country while the Yanks are putting up their tents in Merry Old England. They've got lots of money and loads of time to chase after your women.

And what about you?

◀ ▲ Two German propaganda leaflets dropped in Italy and meant for British troops away from home. They were intended to demoralise the soldiers and cause trouble between the British and their American allies.

The most famous of Germany's propagandists was American-born William Joyce. He emphasised certain words in a peculiar way, which led to his being nicknamed 'Lord Haw-Haw'. Joyce tried to give the impression that he knew exactly what was going on in Britain. This was fine when his information was correct but made him look foolish when, as often happened, he was wrong. As a result, his broadcasts from Germany soon became a source of amusement rather than information or fear. Nevertheless, after the war Joyce was arrested, found guilty of treason and hanged in London in January 1946.

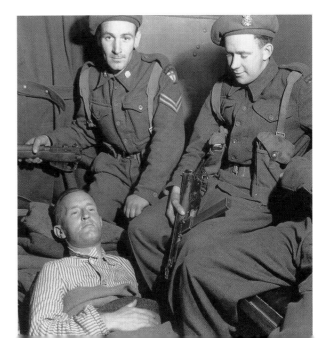

▶ William Joyce, – 'Lord Haw-Haw' – under guard while being taken to hospital. He had been shot and wounded while being captured on the German/Danish border.

Secrets and Spies

▲ Odette Hallowes was one of Britain's most famous World War Two spies.

▼ ▶ There were many posters to remind people that spies might be listening, and that careless chatter could risk the lives of servicemen and women.

In the early years of the war the British were obsessed with the idea of enemy spies in their midst. Odette Hallowes, who had lived for most of her life in France, was immediately suspicious after responding to the War Office request to the public for photographs of the French coast:

'To my amazement, I got a letter asking if I would go to London to be interviewed. I thought ... I am going to get my photographs back. So I went, and they talked to me, but nothing really was said ... I forgot about it until some time later I was asked to go back again. Then I got very cross, because when I arrived, the officer who was going to question me said, "We are very pleased. We have found out all about your background in France."

'I said, "Wait a minute, what do you think I am, a spy or what?"'

Odette was about to be asked to spy for Britain in France! She accepted, but was captured and endured the most terrible hardships in Ravensbruck concentration camp, in Germany.

Both British and German propaganda fed the anxiety about spies. The Germans pretended to broadcast from Britain, and announced that their spies would be dressed as miners. In fact, only a few German spies ever came to the country and nearly all were so obviously strangers that they were arrested at once.

▲ Although posters like this urged people not to talk about the war to strangers, there were actually very few German spies in Britain and almost no war secrets were revealed to them.

◀ Workers of the Roads Department remove signs that might be of assistance to enemy invaders.

'Most of you know your policemen and your ARP wardens by sight. If you keep your heads you can also tell whether a military officer is really British or is only pretending to be.'

Government pamphlet, June 1940

A Poet's Advice by A.P. Herbert, May 1940

'Do not believe the tale the milkman tells;
No troops have mutinied at Potters Bar.
Nor are there submarines at Tunbridge Wells.
The BBC will warn us when there are.'

▶ Dull instruction leaflets like this one, published in 1940, were seen as boring and often left unread.

WAS IT WORTH IT?

PUT OUT YOUR PAPER FOR SALVAGE

▲ The Ministry of Information backed up posters like this with the flattering words: 'The housewife has the warm satisfaction of knowing how directly her sacrifice of energy and triumphs of ingenious makeshift contribute to the war.'

At its largest the Ministry of Information employed 3,000 people. Other ministries employed a further 1,700 staff on propaganda work. The budget for all propaganda purposes has never been worked out, but it ran into many millions of pounds. Was it all worth it?

Did anyone believe extraordinary stories like this?
'A plane trap erected by the Ministry of Transport caught a German bomber yesterday and wrecked it. All the crew were killed. The trap is the latest British "hush-hush" defence weapon ...'

Daily Mirror, 16 August 1940

Like advertising today, it is very difficult to gauge the success of wartime propaganda. Over the summer and autumn of 1940 the mood of the country changed from one of despair to one of dogged determination: propaganda, led by Churchill's speeches, certainly helped in this change.

▼ A British Government poster from early in the war. It was not very popular because people did not like being ordered to 'fight for it now', and the majority of them lived in crowded towns and cities, not pretty villages like this.

Your BRITAIN · fight for it now

◀ *Everyone was encouraged
to help with the war effort.
These schoolchildren in a
village near Canterbury,
in Kent, helped with
war savings.*

Furthermore, Britain managed to persuade more people to help in the war effort than any other warring nation. Propaganda certainly played a part in building this national unity, though precisely how large a part we will never know.

Through wartime surveys and opinion polls the Government found out more about the population than had ever been known before. It learned to guide people by clever campaigns and, where possible, change its policies to meet their needs. These new skills were carried on into the post-war world.

After 1945 the Labour and Conservative Parties used the lessons of wartime propaganda. Having altered their policies they persuaded voters that they were offering them just what they wanted. This was best shown in the Conservative Party after its heavy defeat in the general election of 1945. It changed itself radically, returned to power in 1951 and remained in government until 1964.

▶ *Was this the most successful propaganda sentence of all time?
The words of Churchill's famous Battle of Britain speech were
used over and over again in all kinds of propaganda.*

"NEVER WAS SO MUCH OWED BY SO MANY TO SO FEW" THE PRIME MINISTER

GLOSSARY

Act A law.

air-raid shelter A place where people could shelter from a bomb attack. Many were underground.

Allies, the Britain, France, the USA, Russia and other countries that fought against Germany, Italy and Japan in World War Two.

armaments Weapons of war.

armed forces The army, navy and air force.

arms Weapons, usually small, hand-held ones.

black-out, the The Government ordered that no light was to show outside after dark in case it guided an enemy bomber to its target.

Blitz Heavy bombing of a city. 'Blitz' comes from the German word *blitzkrieg* which means 'lightning war'.

call up An expression which means the same as conscript.

censor To control what is said or shown in a book, film, newspaper, etc, by removing certain words or pictures.

civil Of the state.

civil defence The entire organisation of the home front.

civilians Those people not in the armed forces.

Cockney A person from the East End of London, born 'within the sound of Bow Bells'.

conscript To require someone to join the forces or do other war work.

conspire To plan or agree on something in secret.

correspondent A reporter.

democracy A system that allows people to choose their own government.

Dunkirk The Channel port from which the defeated British Expeditionary Force was rescued in May–June 1940.

export To sell goods to another country.

front line The battle line nearest the enemy.

gas mask A mask that fits over the mouth and nose. It filters out poisonous gases in the air.

general election When people vote to decide who will be the government.

Gestapo The Nazi secret police with a reputation for great cruelty.

import To bring in goods from another country.

invade To move into another country by force. In 1940 the Germans invaded France and planned to invade Britain.

media Newspapers, TV, radio and other means of mass communication with the public.

Ministry A government department, e.g. Ministry of Food.

munitions Weapons and ammunition.

Nazi Party Germany's National Socialist Party. It was led by Adolf Hitler and followed his ideas and wishes.

neutral countries Countries which did not take sides in the war.

patriotic Eager to do what is best for one's country.

post war After the war.

radar A machine that uses radio waves for detecting distant objects, such as aircraft, before they are close enough to be seen.

rations The amount of food and other goods people were allowed to buy. It made sure that everyone had an equal share of these items.

rear-guard action A desperate attempt to avoid defeat.

recruit A person who has recently joined a service or job.

resistance movement The secret organisation that formed to fight the German occupying forces in France and other European countries.

slogan A catchy phrase.

swastika The emblem of the Nazi Party.

tap To listen in on someone else's telephone line.

voluntary Something one can choose to do – or not.

warden A person who looks after others. For example, an air-raid warden helped people during air raids.

war savings Money people were urged to save. These savings were used by the Government for the war effort.

PROJECTS ON PROPAGANDA IN WORLD WAR TWO

Find as many pictures of World War Two posters as you can. Take photocopies of them and, where possible, arrange them in the order in which they originally appeared. Study the posters carefully and explain how propaganda posters changed between 1939 and 1945. You might look at issues such as their subject and use of humour. You will find, for example, that many early posters were about the black-out, while many of the later ones were about rationing and saving food. Why was this?

Devise your own piece of World War Two propaganda. It can be in any form, from a poster to a speech to be delivered on the radio.

A project on propaganda during World War Two needs information from various sources. Sources produced at the time of the war are sometimes called *primary* and those produced since that time are sometimes called *secondary*. Some more recent sources of information, mainly books and websites, are listed on the next page. They give mostly other people's views about the war. Sources from the time of war itself are like the quotations in this book. They make a project really interesting and original.

Here are some ways to find primary information:

- Talking to people who lived through the war.
- Looking for objects remaining from the time of the war. These can be large things like buildings. For example, is there an air-raid shelter still standing near you? Smaller objects include steel helmets and gas masks.
- Visiting museums. Most local museums have excellent displays about their area during World War Two. National museums, like the Imperial War Museum in London, are packed with fascinating information.
- Looking at old photographs in family albums.
- Reading printed memories. Your local library will probably have collections made from your area.
- Visit websites that contain primary information, but read the warning on the next page first!

FURTHER INFORMATION

BOOKS TO READ

At Home In World War Two: At Work, Stewart Ross (Evans, 2004)
At Home In World War Two: The Blitz, Stewart Ross (Evans, 2002)
At Home In World War Two: Evacuation, Stewart Ross (Evans, 2002)
At Home In World War Two: Rationing, Stewart Ross (Evans, 2002)
At Home In World War Two: Women's War, Stewart Ross (Evans, 2002)
Coming Alive! The Second World War: Dear Mum, I Miss You! Stewart Ross (Evans, 2001)
Coming Alive! The Second World War: What If the Bomb Goes Off? Stewart Ross (Evans, 2001)
History in Writing: The Second World War, Christine Hatt (Evans, 2000)
Home Front 1939–1945: Propaganda, Fiona Reynoldson (Wayland, 1991)
In Grandma's Day: War, Faye Gardner (Evans, 2000)
Investigating the Home Front, Alison Honey, (National Trust, 1996)

WEBSITES

Just because information is on the web, it does not mean it is true. Well-known organisations like the BBC, a university or the Imperial War Museum have sites you can trust. If you are unsure about a site, ask your teacher.

Here are a few useful sites (all are http:// or http://www.):
bbc.co.uk/history/wwtwo.shtml
historyplace.com/worldwar2
angelfire.com/la/reader/England.html
iwm.org.uk/lambeth/lambeth.htm

Picture acknowledgements
The following images are courtesy of the Imperial War Museum. Figures following page numbers refer to photograph negative numbers: Cover and imprint page poster: PST3718, cover (centre): D1713, cover (background): HU56139, title page: HU36254, contents page: D5598, p.4: KY12227, p.5 (top): HU36119, p.5 (bottom): PST2916, p.6 (top): PST3108, p.6 (bottom): D12029, p.7 (inset): HU3341, p.7 (main picture): HU28292, p.8 (top): H1655, p.8 (bottom): PST0761, p.9 (top): KY12139D, p.9 (bottom): PST3107, p.10: CH15332, p.11 (top): D1303, p.11 (bottom): Dept of Printed Papers, p.12 (top): HU56139, p.12 (bottom): HU36253, p.13 (top): H5600, p.13 (bottom): Dept of Art Road & Rail Section, p.14 (top): PST3750, p.15 (top): HU3194, p.15 (bottom): D1713, p.16 (top): Dept of Art, Health Section, p.16 (bottom left): PST3374, p.16 (bottom right): MH13260. p.17 (top): D20378, p.17 (centre): HU36203, p.17 (bottom right): LDP288, p.18: CH15492, p.19 (top): OWIL29629, p.19 (bottom): EA29623, p.20 (top): H20446, p.20 (bottom): D17908, p.21 (top): A21269, p.21 (bottom): P551, p.22 (top): D2972, p.22 (bottom): D12912, p.23 (top): PST2948, p.23 (bottom): D13210, p.24: A6192, p.25 (top): HU68842, p.25 (centre): HU68867, p.25 (bottom): BU6911, p.26 (top): HU3213, p.26 (bottom left): PST0694, p.26 (bottom right): PST3363, p.27 (top right): PST0693, p.27 (centre): HU49251, p.27 (bottom): LDP230, p.28 (top): 4947, p.28 (bottom): PST3640, p.29 (top): D5022, p.29 (bottom): PST0026. Cartoon on page 14 courtesy of Mirrorpix.

Sources of quoted material
Pages 13 (bottom), 20 (bottom) and 24 (centre left): Personal interviews with author.
Page 8: Taken from Winston S. Churchill, *The Second World War, vol. 2: Their Finest Hour,* Penguin, 1985, p.104.
Page 9 (centre): Taken from Raynes Minns, *Bombers and Mash The Domestic Front 1939–45,* Virago, 1999, p.36.
Page 9 (bottom): As above, p.91.

Page 10: Taken from Winston S. Churchill, *The Second World War, vol. 2: Their Finest Hour,* Penguin, 1985, p.151.
Page 13 (centre): Quote in Ministry of Information book taken from Fiona Reynoldson, *The Home Front 1939–1945: Propaganda,* Wayland, 1991, p.9.
Page 14: Taken from Mavis Nicholson, ed., *What Did You Do In the War, Mummy?* Chatto and Windus, 1995, pp.209–10.
Page 17 (top): Taken from Raynes Minns, *Bombers and Mash The Domestic Front 1939–45,* Virago, 1999, p.91.
Page 17; *Daily Mail* government notice taken from: Raynes Minns, *Bombers and Mash The Domestic Front 1939–45,* Virago, 1999, p.142.
Page 18: Taken from in Fiona Reynoldson, *Home Front 1939–1945: Propaganda,* Wayland, 1991, p.21.
Page 19: Taken from Raynes Minns, *Bombers and Mash The Domestic Front 1939–45,* Virago, 1999, p.194.
Page 20 (top): Taken from *Ourselves in Wartime,* Odhams, p.206.
Page 20 (centre): As above, p.209.
Page 21: Wilfred Pickles quote taken from Angus Calder, *The People's War Britain 1939–1945,* Pimlico, 1992, p.504.
Page 21: Lil Lawrence quote taken from Fiona Reynoldson, *The Home Front 1939–1945: Propaganda,* Wayland, 1991, p.19.
Page 22: As above, p.10.
Page 23 (top right): Letter to local paper taken from Angus Calder, *The People's War Britain 1939–1945,* Pimlico, 1992, p.370.
Page 23 (bottom right): As above, p.367.
Page 24 (top left): Taken from Fiona Reynoldson, *The Home Front 1939–1945: Propaganda,* Wayland, 1991, p.29.
Page 24 (bottom left): As above, p.23.
Page 26: Taken from Mavis Nicholson, ed., *What Did You Do In the War, Mummy?* Chatto and Windus, 1995, p.239.
Page 27 (top): Taken from Angus Calder, *The People's War Britain 1939–1945,* Pimlico, 1992, p.135.
Page 27 (bottom): A.P. Herbert poem cited in Angus Calder, *The People's War Britain 1939–1945,* Pimlico, 1992, p.134.

INDEX

Numbers in **bold** refer to pictures and captions.